D0765147

DRAW ME A STORY

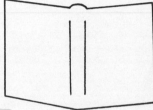

MAY - 1990

Volume   I

By BARBARA FREEDMAN

Feathered Nest Productions, Inc.
Fayetteville, North Carolina

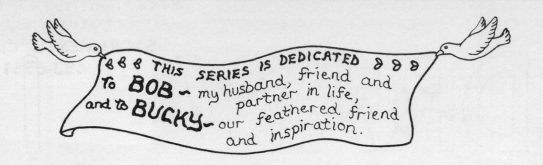

THIS SERIES IS DEDICATED
To BOB — my husband, friend and
partner in life,
and to BUCKY — our feathered friend
and inspiration.

Printed in the United States of America.
ISBN 1-877732-01-X (Volume I)
ISBN 1-877732-00-1 (Series)

Feathered Nest
Productions, Inc.

Feathered Nest Productions, Inc.
Fayetteville, North Carolina

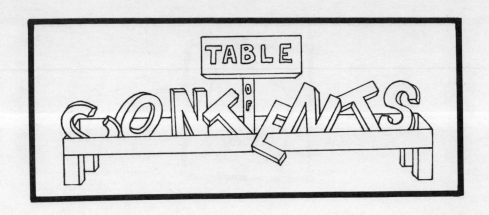

PREFACE   4

INTRODUCTION   5

AFRICAN MASKS OF AGES PAST   10

CAREER TO STEER   14

DAD MAKES ME GLAD   17

FAIRY TALE TIME   21

FITNESS FROLIC   25

MOON TUNE   28

NATURE'S NESTING GROUND   32

PIGS IN A PUDDLE   36

ROBOT ROMP   41

SCHOOL IS COOL   46

SPAIN REIGNS   49

TEDDY BEAR'S WINTER CHEER   52

Welcome to volume I of <u>Draw Me a Story</u>, a collection of tales that have grown out of my experiences as a children's librarian. In designing storyhours and other library programs for children, I have frequently found myself unable to locate draw and tell stories to suit my chosen program themes. As a result, I have been writing more and more of my own tales over the years.

The purpose of this series of books is to share these stories with others, such as librarians, teachers, and parents, who share stories with children. So that the reader can easily determine what each tale is about, the primary subject of a story will always appear as the first word in the story's title. (For example, my story about a teddy bear is entitled, "Teddy Bear's Winter Cheer.")

Therefore, if a specific subject is sought, it can be looked up either in the alphabetically arranged table of contents or in the cumulative title index which will appear in each subsequent volume of this series. I welcome suggestions of topics for possible inclusion in future volumes.

Barbara Freedman

What is a "draw and tell" story? It is a brief tale that is told orally. As characters, objects and actions are described, they are drawn onto a single sheet of paper while an audience looks on. Here is an example, excerpted from one of the stories in volume I, which shows how the drawing builds up as new elements are added.

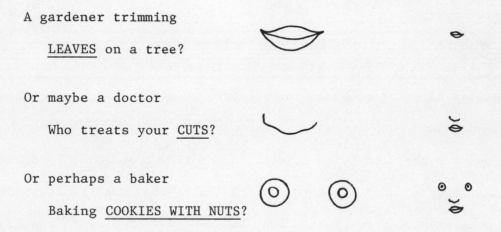

A gardener trimming

   LEAVES on a tree?

Or maybe a doctor

   Who treats your CUTS?

Or perhaps a baker

   Baking COOKIES WITH NUTS?

By the time the story ends, a new object has emerged on the paper from the disparate parts. (In this case it is a human face.) The resulting image summarizes the theme of the story, to the surprise and enjoyment of the watching children. In the above case, the final picture is shown on the following page.

I generally organize each text so that the fragments that are drawn seem to jump around randomly on the page. I save for last the element that will tie all the pieces together. (For example, the outline of a head will unify two eyes, a nose, a mouth, and two ears into a cohesive face.) This makes the final outcome less obvious as the story is being told and allows the storyteller to retain an element of surprise. Because each piece of the picture must function both in its own right, and as a part of the larger picture, every drawing is kept simple and fairly stylized.

So that the performer may quickly spot each instance in which something is to be added to the picture, in the text I have capitalized and underlined each key word. A key word may refer to an object, something symbolized by an object, or a motion that is to be drawn. To the right of each key word is a sketch to show what is to be drawn and a description of the role that the sketch will play in the final composition.

To the right of each sketch fragment is a small depiction of how the overall picture is developing on the storyteller's paper. This allows the performer to see how the total paper should look at each point in the story and to see where each new element should be placed in relation to the rest of the picture.

By highlighting each key word, defining its role in the final picture, and showing how it looks both alone and in relation to the story's outcome, it is hoped that the performance of these tales can be easily mastered by novices and experienced storytellers alike. The layout is designed for ease of use so that the performer may make frequent eye contact with the audience, while easily keeping her or his place in the story. If a word which describes the finished picture is mentioned near the end of the story's text, it too is capitalized and underlined to aid the storyteller by providing emphasis.

Following each tale is a full-size version of its complete drawing. This can be lightly traced, in pencil, onto the paper which will be used during a program. The faint pencil marks will be visible to the storyteller only. They will serve as a guide to the shape and position of each element that is to be drawn during the performance. Then, as the teller tells the tale, each picture fragment is added on with a dark marker. Thus, from the children's perspective, the performer is making up the picture as he or she goes along. A little prior rehearsal will make possible the easy coordination of storytelling and sketching.

For those who are unfamiliar with the concept of a draw and tell story, it may sound forbidding. Actually, the technique is quickly mastered and few materials are required for a performance. These include:

-The text of the draw and tell story

-A large sheet of paper, perhaps in a color that suits the

theme of the tale (such as pink for pigs)

-A pencil, for tracing the image in advance

-A wide-tipped dark marker, for drawing bold lines that can be
seen from a distance by the entire audience

-Tape or tacks, for hanging the paper

-A smooth surface on which to mount the paper (such as a wall
or a flannel board and stand, for example)

-An alternative set of materials could include chalk and a
blackboard.

The draw and tell story is whimsical and unique and well worth
incorporating into many child-oriented activities. Children find humor
and excitement in watching shapes appear before them as they listen to
a tale. Gradually they realize that these shapes are creating a new
composite image. Their critical thinking skills come into play and
they are delighted when they can correctly guess the punchline. They
feel a sense of accomplishment if they can predict the outcome and a
sense of wonder if the end of a story surprises them instead.

The educational and recreational uses of the draw and tell story
are many:

1. Children's librarians have long used this type of story as part
of preschool and school age storytelling sessions. It can add variety
and novelty to a performance and provide a change of pace from book-
centered activities, helping to renew children's interest in the
proceedings.

2. It can serve as an amusing introduction to other activities, such as film viewings or the creation of art projects.

3. In schools and other educational settings, this type of story can be used to peak children's curiosity about a topic which is about to be studied.

4. Parents can share a draw and tell story with their children in a more informal manner during quiet times, along with bedtime stories, or whenever children could do with a little unexpected fun.

5. Such a tale can even perk up a children's party or be used by older children who are baby-sitting or otherwise entertaining younger ones.

A draw and tell story is easy to use, requires no elaborate materials or preparations, and can create fun anytime. Within the library, the school, the community social center, or the home, children may be asking their care-givers to "Draw me a story."

Now let us travel

    On a journey,

To a land steeped

    In mystery.

Down RIVERS

    Overhung with vines,   (forehead)

Through a land

    Of mighty PYRAMIDS,   (nose)

Land a glittering

    DIAMONDS,   (eyes)

10

Land of GRASSY,

    Windblown savannahs,

(hair)

Land of mighty

    HORNED rhinoceros,

(horns)

Land of delicate

    Jungle FLOWERS,

(mouth)

Land of powerful SUN

    Which scorches desert sands,

(mask outline)

Land of sparkling

    Blue LAKES,

(face)

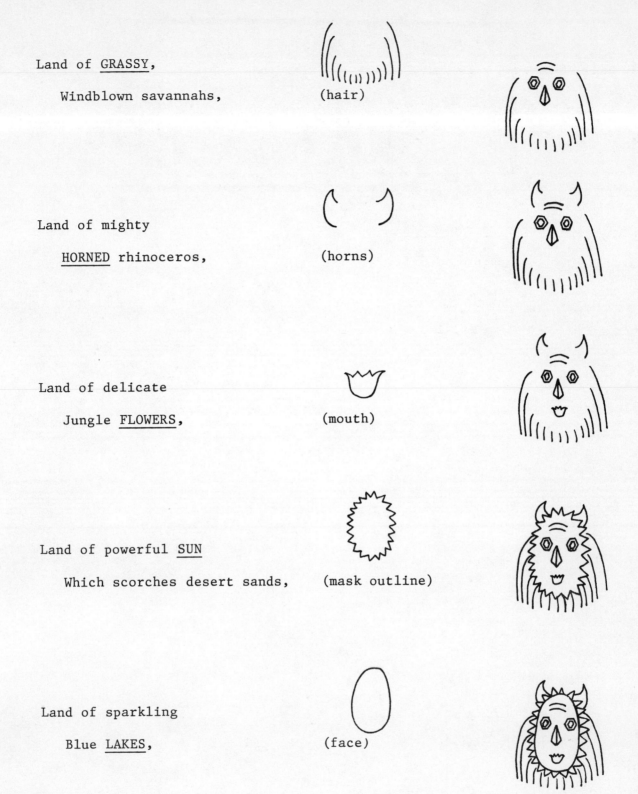

Land of beauty,

    We wish to visit Africa,

The land where sacred <u>MASKS</u>

    Dance the secrets of life.

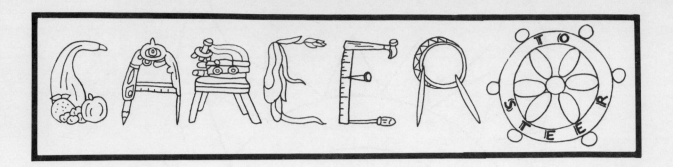

When I grow up,

What shall I be?

A gardener trimming

LEAVES on a tree?   (mouth)

Or maybe a doctor

Who treats your CUTS?   (nose)

Or perhaps a baker

Baking COOKIES WITH NUTS?   (eyeballs)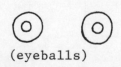

A librarian sharing

   Great <u>BOOKS</u> with you?   (collar)

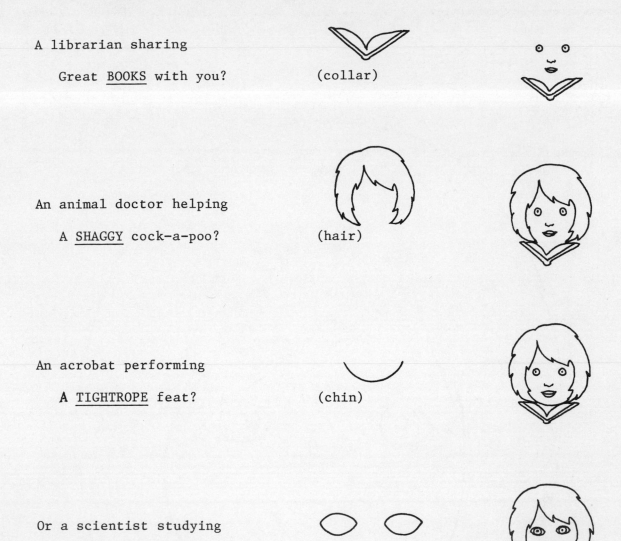

An animal doctor helping

   A <u>SHAGGY</u> cock-a-poo?   (hair)

An acrobat performing

   A <u>TIGHTROPE</u> feat?   (chin)

Or a scientist studying

   <u>PLANETS</u>' heat?   (eyes)

Oh, I'm not sure

   What I might be,

But whatever it is,

   I'll always be me!

I love my dad,

    He's never sad.

Though he works hard all day,

    He's still happy to play.

He bakes

    CUPCAKES,   (feet)

He watches

    Wild SNAKES.   (mouth)

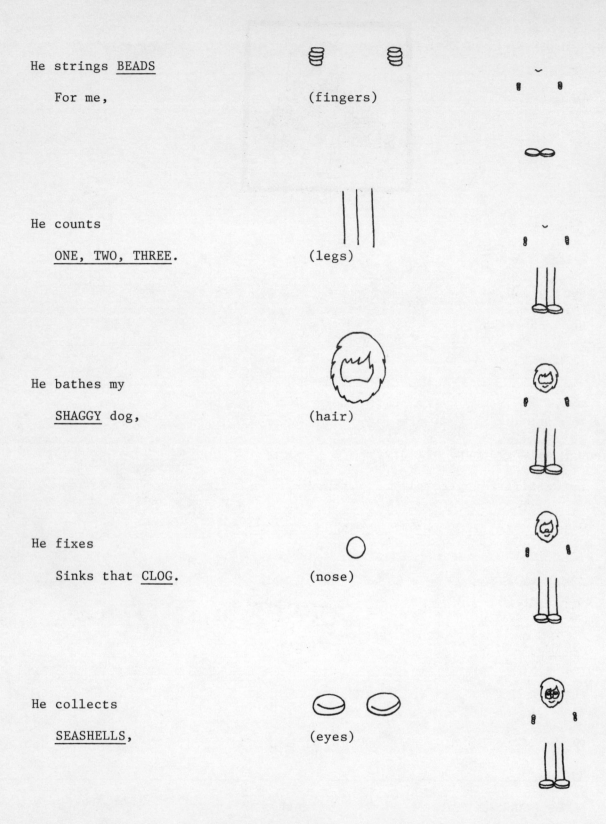

He strings <u>BEADS</u>

   For me,   (fingers)

He counts

   <u>ONE, TWO, THREE</u>.   (legs)

He bathes my

   <u>SHAGGY</u> dog,   (hair)

He fixes

   Sinks that <u>CLOG</u>.   (nose)

He collects

   <u>SEASHELLS</u>,   (eyes)

And great stories

    He tells.

Oh, when he reads

    A <u>BOOK</u> to me,   (book)

I'm just as happy

    As I can be.

I love my <u>DAD</u>

    And I have found

That he can make

    My world go round.

19

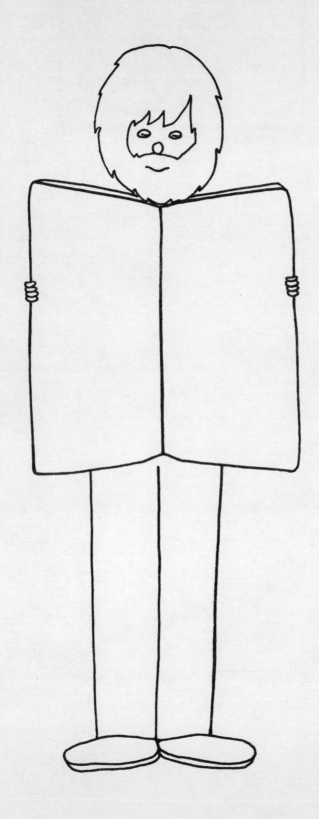

Here are the three CHAIRS

    Of the three bears,   (tower tops)

And here by the floor

    Is Red Riding Hood's DOOR.   (door)

And Sleeping Beauty's FINGER

    Pricked for she lingered,   (right tower)

Rapunzel's TOWER

    Where she waited by the hour,   (middle tower)

Snow White's <u>COFFIN</u>,

    Visited often.

 (drawbridge)

Here is the top <u>MATTRESS</u>

    Of the princess

    In her blue dress,

 (cloud)

While here is the <u>WALL</u>

    From which Humpty

    Dumpty will fall

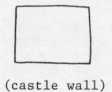 (castle wall)

And bits of his <u>SHELL</u>

    After he fell.

 (windows)

So where do we draw

    The common line

Among these fairy tales

From once upon a time?

They're stories that are

Often told aloud,

All made up in a <u>CASTLE</u>

<u>UPON A CLOUD</u>.

There are lots
    Of ways to exercise,
We can each pick one
    To fit our lives.

Oh, a hopscotch <u>GRID</u>
    Is lots of fun   (netting)

Or you may prefer
    To hit a <u>HOME RUN</u>.   (ball)

By swinging a <u>BAT</u>
    Forward and back   (handle)

Or perhaps you'd rather

    Jog around a <u>TRACK</u>.   (frame)

A <u>JUMPROPE</u> workout

    Can keep you fit   (stitching)

But, whatever you do,

    You must never quit!

Now, what do you think

    My favorite could be?

Why, it's clearly <u>TENNIS</u>,

    Indubitably!

Once there was a lonely little
star. It TWINKLED weakly
and was so sad.   (eyelid)

It wanted a friend. It wanted
one so badly that it set
out ACROSS the universe.   (eyelash)

It wandered IN AND OUT of
galaxies,   (chin)

And around many CORNERS, past
lots of solar systems.   (upper lip)

It fell in and out of

black <u>HOLES</u>.   (lower lip)

It <u>SWERVED</u> around giant

suns, crowded by circling

planets.   (nose)

It slid in and out of gravity

fields and wafted through

time warps, and <u>GLIDED</u>

past a comet.   (forehead)

At long last it saw one whom

it knew could be its

friend, so it zipped

<u>AROUND</u> the planet earth to

reach it.   (back)

Do you know who this friend

was?

It was the <u>MOON</u>!

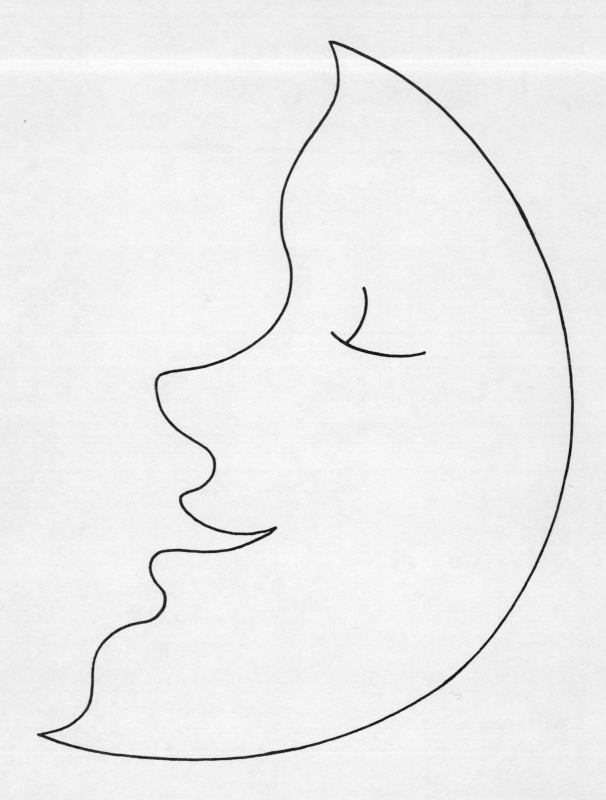

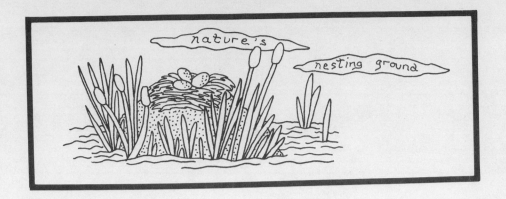

The natural world

   Tries to survive.

In the twentieth century

   It's barely alive.

BULLETS fly as

   People hunt and kill

And slaughter the wild

   Animals at will.

(hole in tree)

POLLUTION pours from the

   Factory smokestack,

Choking the air and

   Making us hack.

(foliage)

32

Bulldozers come and

    TEAR up the land,

Turning once fertile

    Valleys to sand.

(bird's body)

For the earth

    To mend,

The madness

    Must end.

We must

    Nurture life

And stop

    Creating strife.

We need to clean up

    Every toxic heap;

The earth requires

    A thorough SWEEP.

(trunk)

Did I hear you say,

    "Who holds the <u>KEY</u>?"

Every single person,

    Including you and me!   (bird's head)   

It is our duty

    To make the earth well,

And once again a home

    Where we can safely dwell.

We'll rebuild a planet

    With lots of green spaces

And <u>SHRUBS</u> for nesting      

    In quiet places.   (nest)

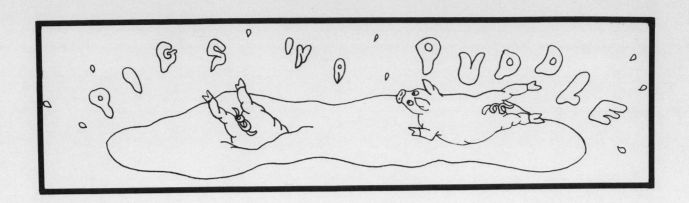

In a big

    plot of <u>DIRT</u>,

    <u>TWO FRIENDS</u>

    played one day.

(head)

(eyes)

But they felt

    very sleepy

    after chewing

    on some <u>HAY</u>.

(eyeballs)

They lay down

    to take a nap,

    and soon they

    closed their eyes.

And later,

    when they woke up,

    they got

    a big surprise!

For as they'd slept

    the rain had come,

    it poured and

    poured and poured.

Then it slowed

    down to a drip,

    <u>RAINDROPS</u> fell

    as they snored.

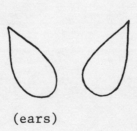 (ears)

Well, such a lovely

    mud <u>PUDDLE</u>

    had formed

    during the storm,

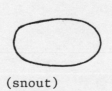 (snout)

That they waddled

    over to it,

    to see if

    it was warm.

It felt so good

    and squooshy

    that they had to

    <u>DIVE</u> right in,

(nostrils)

And ever since

    that moment —

    in that puddle

    they have been!

Who finds the mud

    so soothing

    to skin that

    gets too dry?

Why these two

little PIGGIES.

Why don't you

give it a try?

40

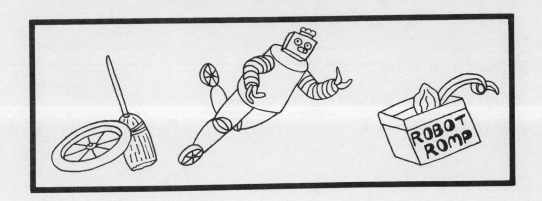

One day, I went down into my
    cellar.

I was tired of cleaning up
    my room and wanted to see
    if there was anything
    that could help save me
    some work.

I dug around through some junk
    and tossed FOUR BOXES aside
    to get at some scraps of
    metal that were at the
    bottom of the pile of junk.

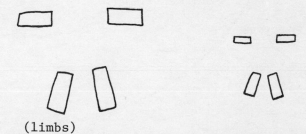

(limbs)

I found some great GADGETS: all
sorts of old knobs and dials
and shiny handles.

(face and panel dials)

I built a wooden STAND and set
up some of the knobs on top
of it so that it looked
really neat.

(chest panel)

Then I bent and unbent a big
piece of METAL until I
got it all smoothed out.

(head)

Next I took some loose WIRES
and used them to rig up a
BATTERY.

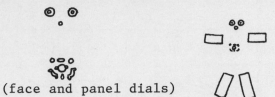

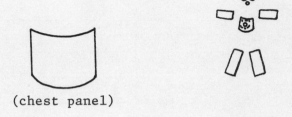

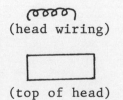

(head wiring)

(top of head)

That battery could operate

TWO SCOOPS that might

pick toys up from the

floor of my room.   (hands)

I was so lucky that day,

because I even found some

old doll carriage WHEELS

that would make my cleanup

machine easy to roll into

the bedroom.   (feet)

But I still needed something

to tie all my great parts

together so I dug and dug

through a pile in the

corner of the basement.

And then I found it - a
rusty old <u>BARREL</u> that I
could salvage.

(body)

It would make the perfect
body for my Roving Room-
Restoring <u>ROBOT</u>!

Where can you go

    To learn to add?

What's <u>TWO PLUS TWO?</u>

    <u>FOUR</u> can't be bad.

(math problem)

Where can you go

    To learn to read?

<u>LINE BY LINE</u>

    With great speed?

(base)

Where can you go

    To learn to write?

Straight <u>UP</u> and <u>DOWN</u>,

    Hold your pencil tight.

(edges of base)

Where can you go

    To learn of nature?

Of worms that crawl

    And <u>CATS</u> that purr?   (sketch of cat)

Where can you go

    To learn history,

Hear picture <u>BOOKS</u>,

    Be told a story?   (chalk eraser)

Where can you go

    To learn your shapes?

<u>SQUARES</u> make boxes

    And circles make grapes.   (frame)

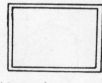 

So where can you go

    To learn all of this?

To school, of course,

    Where the <u>BLACKBOARD</u> sits!

She dances flamenco,

    Its secrets she knows,

Dancing 'round the fire

    Which sparks and glows.

The LOGS on the fire

    Crackle and pop,

And warm the night air,

    A chill to stop.

(frame)

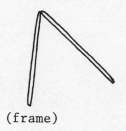

Her CASTANETS click as

    Her hand keeps the beat

And she stamps the ground

    With her forceful feet.

(handle)

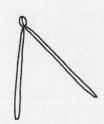

49

And her <u>HAIR</u>, dark and shiny,

    Is wildly flowing.

As she spins ever faster,

    Her movement keeps growing.   (tassels)

Her skirt's soft fabric

    Is <u>RIPPLING</u> and whirling,

Then falling in swirls

    As she stops her twirling.   (folds)

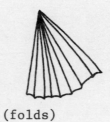 

While high above her head

    Her other hand holds

The beautiful Spanish <u>FAN</u>,

    With all of its folds.

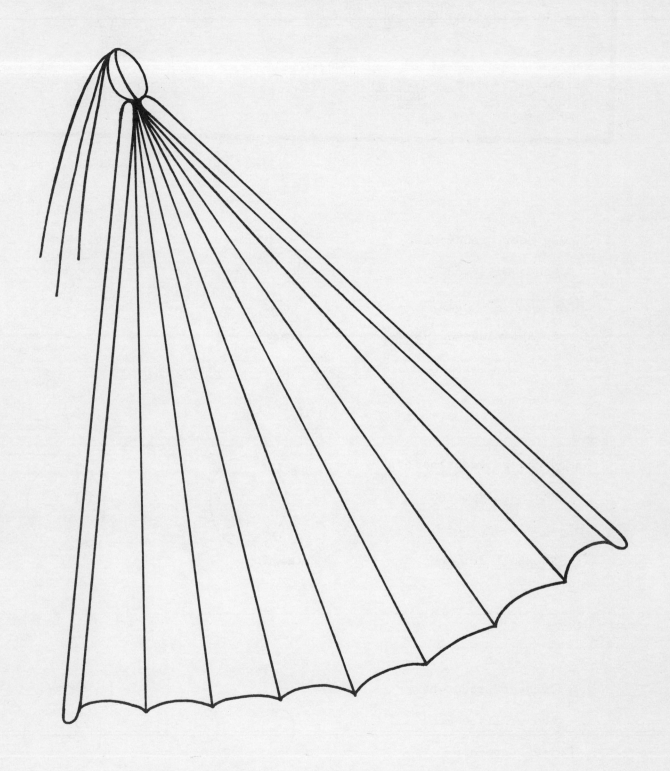

Teddy bear, teddy bear,

    Where will you go?

I'll go out to play

    In the flakes of <u>SNOW</u>.

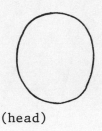

(face)

Teddy bear, teddy bear,

    What will you do?

I'll roll a giant

    <u>SNOWBALL</u> for you.

(head)

Teddy bear, teddy bear,

    Who will you meet?

A giant snowman

    With two big <u>FEET</u>.

(ears)

Teddy bear, teddy bear,

    How will you eat?

I'll bake snow COOKIES

    For a treat.

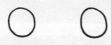

(inner ears)

Teddy bear, teddy bear,

    Why make no sound?

My PAWS PATTER gently

    Over the ground.

(buttonholes)

Teddy bear, teddy bear,

    When will you be home?

When the SNOWDRIFTS melt

    And the stars have shone.

(mouth)

Feathered Nest
Productions, Inc.